☐ NATIONAL GEOGRAPHIC SOCIETY

DESTINATION
Deep Sea

by Jonathan Grupper

NATIONAL GEOGRAPHIC SOCIETY
WASHINGTON, D.C.

W iggle your toes. Yep, they're still there inside those flippers. Slip on that dive mask. You're ready for an eyeful. Pop that snorkel in your mouth and waddle on down to where the sand ends. All it's going to take now is a step, a smile, and a splash.

For 97 percent of what's alive on Earth, this is the place. Water covers almost three-quarters of the planet, but we've only explored less than 5 percent of it. Now you're going to change that. You're going to snorkel, scuba, and submarine the sea from top to bottom—from its big blue surface, down, down to its dark depths. And along the way, you're going to discover that the ocean has many different worlds. Each layer has its own incredible story to tell.

Coral Reef, Australia

ick left, kick right, and away you glide across the tropical shallows. The sands beneath you spread on with few signs of life. At last you squint at a strange burst of color ahead. Take a deep breath through your snorkel and down you plunge, 15 feet to a coral reef.

This is a city undersea, bustling with activity, thanks to an animal no bigger than the tip of your pinky. It's called a coral polyp, and, unlike you, its skeleton is on the outside of its body. As each polyp dies, it leaves its casing behind. Over thousands of years, millions build upon millions, creating a vast undersea colony that draws a dazzling variety of marine life.

To blend with the sunlit reef, butterflyfish change colors. Clownfish dart amid anemones, immune to their poison. A parrotfish emerges from a bubble of mucus that sealed off its smell from nighttime predators. In this crowded realm, every creature has its own elaborate strategy to survive.

Butterflyfish

Coral Reef

Parrotfish in Mucus Bubble

Pufferfish with Coral Fan

Clownfish in Anemone

*B*rrrrr. You're hundreds of miles away, and you've traded those tropical waters for temperate ones. You're piloting a dive boat, and who's that squealing playfully in its wake? *Click, click, click.* It's a pod of one of the friendliest and most intelligent mammals in the sea. The dolphin isn't a fish, it's an air-breather, like you. Dolphins can stay underwater for only a few minutes at a time, and now, down into the ocean they go. If you want to join them, you'd better suit up with some serious gear.

You speed along, heading north, then cut your engine. Between that weight belt, the wet suit, and the heavy tank on your back, you feel like you can barely stand up. But take a test breath through your regulator, take a step off the deck, and take off. You're flying.

Go on, give it a try. Spread your arms, kick your feet, and fly through the water. Tuck and turn, do a loop-the-loop, go for a somersault. You're an aquanaut floating through space. It's called scuba—self-contained underwater breathing apparatus. And if you didn't need that mouth-piece to breathe, you'd let out a holler.

By now those dolphins have headed back to the surface to catch their breath. But thanks to your tank, you can dive on. The adventure is just beginning.

Long-Beaked Common Dolphins

California Sea Otter

A furry swimmer slips past. Hurry now, go follow that otter. Through a swirling school of anchovy fish. Past the towering columns of an undersea kelp forest. Down, 40 feet, to the urchin beds that spread below.

What are urchins? They're spiky balls that look like living pincushions—though to the otter they look like breakfast. The otter swoops down to snatch one up, tucks its prize into a fold of skin behind its foreleg, and speeds back to the surface. Floating on its back, the otter props a flat rock on its chest and pounds the urchin until it cracks open. Yum. Breakfast is ready!

If you think urchins are oddballs, wait until you meet their closest cousins.

Kelp Forest

Sea Urchins

9

Starfish, or sea stars, never move—or so you might think. Imagine you could speed up time, like in a movie. You'd see those slowpokes scurrying about the seafloor like ants. In fact, every direction is forward to them. They have eyes on the tip of each arm. They have no face and no brain. To eat, some sea stars stick their stomach into their food, not the other way around.

The ocean is a place where normal is what isn't normal.

Still, not everyone lives in slow motion. Fast as it can snap its claws, a hermit crab steals the larger shell of another crab. And off the loser scurries to find a shell of its own to claim.

The winner hunkers down, safe in its snug, new home. It's a whole different world for those that live out in the open ocean.

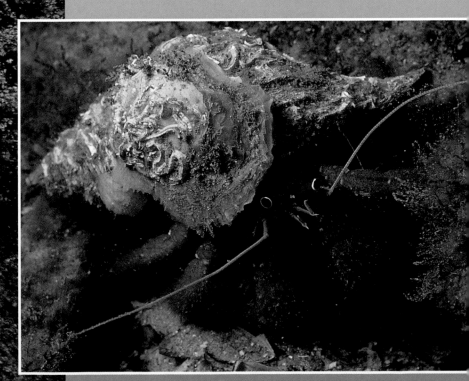

Hermit Crab

Whale Shark

They sweep past you by the thousands. But have no fear. A hammerhead's teeth are small by shark standards. Its real secret weapon stretches across its broad head—an arsenal of tiny organs that are so sensitive they can detect the heartbeat of a passing fish.

There are more than 350 kinds of sharks, from the velvet belly lanternshark, which is no longer than your forearm, to the massive whale shark—at seven times your size, the largest fish in the world. Sharks roam in every ocean, and most wouldn't even have a taste for the likes of you. Some eat plankton, tiny morsels of living matter adrift in the currents.

Out here in the open ocean, before you can eat something, you have to hunt it down.

Hammerhead Sharks

Velvet Belly Lanternshark

Just when you're thinking life here couldn't get any stranger, take a look at what lives 60 feet down. The *mola mola,* it's called, and it's weird weird. It can grow to be as big as a car, and it's just as custom-made for cruising. Its great fins work like oars, and that big ball of a body is streamlined to glide.

Actually, you're not the only one who's stopped to admire the *mola mola* body. *Penella filosa* is a parasite, an animal that feeds off another animal's body. And to it, the *mola mola* is a floating buffet. The parasite clings to it, savoring the juicy muscles of the *mola mola*'s big fins.

And what, you ask, does the *mola mola* eat? Dive on and find out.

School of *Mola Mola*

Parasitic Copepod

Diver with *Mola Mola*

They say you are what you eat, and the *mola mola*'s meal seems just as strange as *it* is! Moon jellyfish gather in schools that can stretch for miles. Maybe you've seen jellies washed up on the beach, looking like big globs of goo. But watching one glide gracefully through the currents, you'd think it was dancing an underwater ballet.

Box Jellyfish

School of Moon Jellyfish

Sea Nettle

As it opens and shuts its dome, a jelly propels itself through the water. Each of its tentacles is barbed with thousands of tiny harpoons that fire on contact. Together, they form a mesh that spreads long and wide, snaring tiny shrimp and fish. Be careful—don't swim too close. One type, the box jellyfish, is the most poisonous creature on the planet.

The deeper something goes, the more pressure it feels from the water above. Some jellyfish are designed to descend thousands of feet without getting crushed. But if you want to dive farther, you'd better trade in your scuba gear....

Seventy feet, 80 feet. You are piloting a one-person submersible, a kind of deep-sea scooter, into waters unknown. You can see clearly in every direction—until you reach 100 feet, where darkness begins to descend on the ocean. Welcome to the twilight zone. Here, there's less sunlight, which means fewer plants and less oxygen for marine life to breathe. What could survive down here? Flip on your lights and find out.

It's called marine snow—the shower of minute debris that sinks through the water. It's made of decaying stuff from the surface as well as the tiny creatures that feast off it. Awaiting the banquet with open arms— eight, to be exact—is a pelagic octopus. To collect its meal, it simply drops through it like a parachute, swiping morsels along the way.

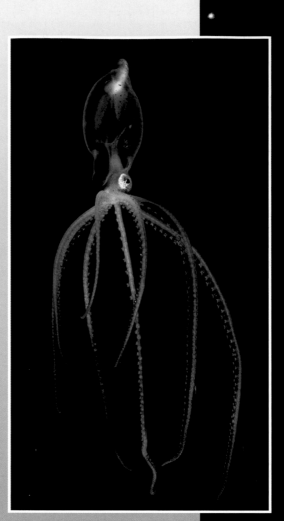

Pelagic Octopus

You're dropping, too—down to 1,000 feet, the waters that are home to a fabled creature. The giant squid can grow to be as long as two school buses, and its eyes are as large as hubcaps, yet no one has ever seen one in the wild. For now, out of the gloom appears a smaller cousin, aglow.

Animals down here come equipped with their own flashlights. Turn off your sub's headlights and watch the deep come alive.

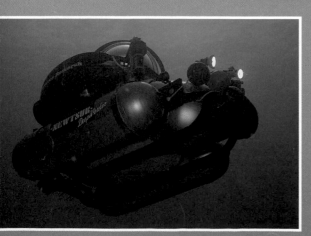

Submersible

Squid with Marine Snow

Even their names sound creepy: fangtooth, black devil, dragonfish, viperfish. Surviving at 2,000 feet is enough to drive anyone to extremes. But living in the midnight zone does have one appeal: Predators are few and far between. Then again, finding prey in the dark takes some doing as well.

Some midnight zone fish have ultrasensitive eyes, attuned to the gloom. Some fish glow in the dark and are studded with tiny lights called photophores. Others come equipped with their own flashlight stalks sprouting from their foreheads. Some dangle lit fishing lures from their chins, an irresistible beacon in the darkness. Many have teeth so long they actually pierce the roof of their own mouth.

Think you've gone deep enough? You've hardly scratched the ocean's surface.

Omosudis

Fangtooth

Dragonfish

Anglerfish

Black Devil

Tuna Crabs

Launching an ROV

Before you is a bank of television screens and computers. Beside you is a crew of marine biologists and engineers. You're taking them to the ocean floor without even getting them wet. That's because you're manning the controls of an ROV—a remotely operated vehicle. It's a robot that relays what it sees to the surface while you stay aboard the ship. Now, suddenly, your screens get clouded by currents thick with dust. Those particles are alive.

A migration is a large group of animals all traveling someplace at once. Some, like the tuna crab, travel from inshore waters to offshore

waters. But the largest migration on Earth occurs every evening across all the world's oceans, as a surge of life rises from the depths of the sea. Krill—millions of tiny shrimplike creatures—come paddling furiously through the water. What draws them is the layer of plant life that skims the ocean's surface, now swollen from a full day of sunlight.

Krill and tuna crabs may be small, but they're food enough for the largest appetite in the world.

Close-Up of Krill

Blue Whale

24

A hush falls over the control room as your ROV's cameras are filled with a breathtaking spectacle: a creature that may weigh 130 tons, as much as 1,700 adult humans. Its tongue is as big as an elephant, and its heart the size of a car. The blue whale is the largest animal that has ever lived on Earth. Every day it filters up to four tons of krill through baleen—massive sieves that line its mouth.

Whales, like sharks, come in all shapes and sizes. There are humpbacks, which sing to communicate. There are orcas, which hunt with their teeth. Gray whales travel 8,000 miles a year to feed and give birth—the longest migration of any mammal.

Like other marine mammals, whales must get to the surface to breathe. But your ROV doesn't need to catch its breath. It's still got a long descent ahead of it.

A Cluster of Tube Worms

Finally, after a long night's search, your sonar sweeps into sharp focus at 6,000 feet. Your temperature gauge jumps from near freezing to 600°F. Across your monitors comes a vision that no one would have imagined only a few years ago: smoke gushing out of the seafloor.

Along the ocean bottom stretches a wide world unseen. There are mountains, valleys, and plains here just like on dry land—all largely unexplored. And just like at Yellowstone, there are some spots where smoke erupts from the ground.

Believe it or not, there are creatures living here too— some that are wholly different life-forms we've only just discovered. Unlike familiar animals that depend on plants and sunlight, these survive on strange chemicals and warm bacteria. Lush gardens of bacteria, tube worms, and giant clams flourish, attracting white crabs and rattail fish.

The average depth of the sea is still double this, at 12,000 feet. And the deepest trench of all hits nearly 36,000 feet—deeper than Mount Everest is high. The ocean is the world's last frontier, a place we know less about than we do about Mars.

Deep–Sea Floor

By the time your ROV has made its long journey back to the ship, the sun is breaking on the surface. Somewhere across these waters otters are reawakening and krill are retreating to the safety of darker depths.

Far from human eyes, a world of wonders awaits our discovery. This is its day, when new technology and new explorers will at last bring the ocean's secrets to light.

A humpback whale bursts through the water, breaching before the bow of your ship. Perhaps it's doing its morning exercises; perhaps it's simply playing. "Come back soon," it seems to say, as now it slips again into the deep.

Tail of a Humpback Whale

A Note from the National Geographic Society

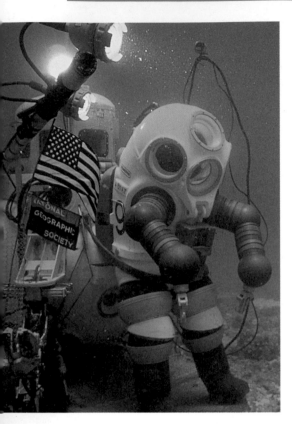

Sylvia Earle Diving in a Jim Suit

Three-quarters of our planet lies hidden beneath the waves. This thick ocean blanket, which moderates Earth's climate and influences its atmosphere, is vital to our survival.

Imagine for a moment we could peel back these precious waters. What might we uncover? Voyaging into the Atlantic, we'd find a massive mountain range longer than the Rockies and Andes combined. As we climbed over this Mid-Atlantic Ridge, we could watch the Earth's crust gush from its central rift valley. Nearing Hawaii, Mauna Kea, the world's highest mountain when measured from the seafloor, would loom ahead. From its submerged base to its lofty summit, this mountain rises thousands of feet higher than Mount Everest. Continuing westward to the Philippine Islands, we could peer into the Mariana Trench. This canyon plunges seven times as deep as the Grand Canyon, making it the steepest, deepest place on Earth.

But the best parts of our oceans lie within their waters, which teem with life. To explore them takes special tools. Since sunlight does not penetrate water effectively, scientists rely heavily on sonar. Sonar stands for sound navigation and ranging. When sound waves are sent through the water to targets like the seafloor, they bounce back. The deeper the seafloor, the longer the echo's return trip. Recording a multitude of echoes allows mapmakers to produce maps that appear quite detailed, but that only hint at what is really there.

Each ocean hosts different varieties of plants and animals. For instance, blackfin tuna *(Thunnus atlanticus)* swim only in the Atlantic while longfin tuna *(Thunnus tongoll)* occur solely in the Pacific. And within the same ocean, different regions exist as well. For example, the world's largest ocean, the Pacific, is warm at the Equator and home to spectacular tropical coral reefs. But travel to the north or south, to California or Chile, and the waters turn cold. Here the waters hold more oxygen and organisms like giant kelp grow as much as one inch a day, creating forests for animals such as rockfish and harbor seals.

But not all cold waters are oxygen rich. No matter what ocean we enter, the deeper we venture from the sunlit surface, the lower the temperature drops. The number of plants as well as the oxygen they produce also decreases with depth. For many years people believed no life could survive under such harsh conditions. Not until scientists began sampling—first with nets, then with submarines and remotely operated vehicles (ROVs)—did views begin to change.

The National Geographic Society has supported hundreds of expeditions to reveal the wealth of life thriving in the deep sea. Recently the Sustainable Seas Expeditions, supported in part by the Society, teamed scientists with submarines to survey the marine life of America's marine sanctuaries. This ambitious project aims to educate the public about the diversity of marine life and the importance of protecting it.

Harbor Seal in a Kelp Forest

We are just now beginning to understand how our actions on the surface can influence life far below. Deep-water environments take much longer to repair themselves than those in the shallows. Projects such as the Sustainable Seas provide important first steps toward maintaining the health of this mysterious submerged world.

Other studies supported by National Geographic are helping answer how life may have started in the seas billions of years ago when Earth was a far less livable place. Some of this work may even help us predict how life might survive on other planets.

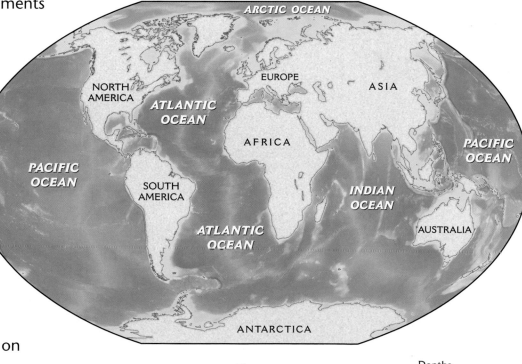

Four great oceans cover the Earth, reaching depths of 36,000 feet.

Depths
- 0–3,000 ft.
- 3,000–5,000 ft.
- 5,000–10,000 ft.
- 10,000–15,000 ft.
- 15,000–20,000 ft.
- 20,000–36,000 ft.

With less than 5 percent of the ocean explored, the most amazing mysteries remain to be discovered right here on our own planet. And they are well within our reach.

What an exciting time to be an explorer headed for the deep sea—the true final frontier!

Published by the
National Geographic Society
1145 17th St. N.W.
Washington, D.C. 20036

John M. Fahey, Jr.
President and Chief
Executive Officer

Gilbert M. Grosvenor
Chairman of the Board

Nina D. Hoffman
Senior Vice President

William R. Gray
Vice President and Director
of the Book Division

Staff for This Book

Nancy Laties Feresten
Director of Children's Publishing

Suzanne Patrick Fonda
Editor

Jennifer Emmett
Associate Editor & Project Editor

Marianne Koszorus
Design Director

Sharon Davis Thorpe
Designer

Janet Dustin
Illustrations Editor

Jo H. Tunstall
Editorial Assistant

Carl Mehler
Director of Maps

XNR Productions,
Gregory Ugiansky
Map Research and Production

Lewis R. Bassford
Production Manager

Vincent P. Ryan
Manufacturing Manager

Illustrations Credits

Cover, Nick Caloyianis/NGS Image Collection; back cover (top left), Stephen Frink/WaterHouse; (top right), Jeff Rotman/Jeff Rotman Photography; (center), Bruce H. Robison; (bottom), Ron Church; endpapers, William R. Curtsinger; 1, Jeff Rotman/Jeff Rotman Photography; 2–3 David Doubilet; 4, F. Stuart Westmoreland; 4–5, Nick Caloyianis/NGS Image Collection; 5 (all), Stephen Frink/WaterHouse; 6–7, Marilyn Kazmers/Innerspace Visions; 8, F. Stuart Westmoreland; 9 (top), David Doubilet; 9 (bottom), Jeff Rotman/Jeff Rotman Photography; 10–11 (both), George Grall/NGS Image Collection; 12, Brian Skerry/NGS Image Collection; 12–13, Paul Humann/Jeff Rotman Photography; 13, Jeff Rotman/Innerspace Visions; 14–15 (all), Mike Johnson; 16 (top), David Doubilet; 16–17, F. Stuart Westmoreland; 17, Mike Johnson; 18 (top), Jeff Rotman/Jeff Rotman Photography; 18 (bottom), Kip Evans; 18–19, Bruce H. Robison; 20–21 (except 21 center), Bruce H. Robison; 21 (center), Darlyne Murawski/NGS Image Collection; 22–23, Maria Stenzel/NGS Image Collection; 23 (top), Maria Stenzel; 23 (bottom), George Mobley; 24–25, Phillip Colla; 26 (top), John R. Dymond; 26, Emory Kristof/NGS Staff; 26–27, Ron Church; 28–29, Michael Melford; 30, Al Giddings Images; 31, David Doubilet; 32, Jeff Rotman/Jeff Rotman Photography.

To my mother, the biggest kid I know—JG

National Geographic would like to thank Tierney Thys for her indispensable consulting and research assistance and for writing the Note from the National Geographic Society.

Library of Congress
Catalog Number:
00-27643

ISBN 0-7922-7693-0

FRONT COVER: Beluga Whale
TITLE PAGE: Butterflyfish
ENDPAPERS: A School of Blue-and-Gold Fusilier

Wolffish

The world's largest nonprofit scientific and educational organization, the National Geographic Society was founded in 1888 "for the increase and diffusion of geographic knowledge." Since then it has supported scientific exploration and spread information to its more than nine million members worldwide.

The National Geographic Society educates and inspires millions every day through magazines, books, television programs, videos, maps and atlases, research grants, the National Geographic Bee, teacher workshops, and innovative classroom materials.

The Society is supported through membership dues and income from the sale of its educational products. Members receive NATIONAL GEOGRAPHIC magazine—the Society's official journal—discounts on Society products, and other benefits.

For more information about the National Geographic Society and its educational programs and publications, please call 1-800-NGS-LINE (647-5463). Visit the Society's Web site: www.nationalgeographic.com